21st Century Basic Skills Library

WE CELEBRATE EARTH DAY IN SPRING

by Jenna Lee Gleisner

Cherry Lake Publishing • Ann Arbor, Michigan

1

Published in the United States of America
by Cherry Lake Publishing
Ann Arbor, Michigan
www.cherrylakepublishing.com

Consultant: Marla Conn, ReadAbility, Inc.

Photo Credits: Fuse/Thinkstock, Cover, Title, 8; Shutterstock Images, 4, 10, 14; Thinkstock, 6, 20; Diego Cervo/Shutterstock Images, 12; Monkey Business Images/Shutterstock Images, 16, 18

Library of Congress Cataloging-in-Publication Data
Gleisner, Jenna Lee.
  We celebrate earth day in spring / by Jenna Lee Gleisner.
     pages cm. -- (Let's look at spring)
Audience: 5-7.
Audience: K to grade 3.
Includes index.
  ISBN 978-1-62431-658-6 (hardcover) -- ISBN 978-1-62431-685-2 (pbk.) -- ISBN 978-1-62431-712-5 (pdf) -- ISBN 978-1-62431-739-2 (hosted ebook)
  1. Earth Day--Juvenile literature. I. Title.

GE195.5.G54 2013
394.262--dc23

                          2013028944

Cherry Lake Publishing would like to acknowledge the work of The Partnership for 21st Century Skills. Please visit *www.p21.org* for more information.

Printed in the United States of America
Corporate Graphics Inc.
January 2014

TABLE OF CONTENTS

Spring Begins

Spring is here. It gets warmer. Plants and trees grow.

What Do You See?

What objects go in the recycle bin?

Earth Day

We have a special day to help our Earth. This day is called Earth Day.

Earth Day is April 22.
People work together
to help our planet.

Celebrate

We **celebrate** Earth Day many ways. One way is to learn about our Earth.

What Do You See?

Where is Lee's class learning?

Lee's class learns about keeping Earth clean. People need clean air and water. Animals do, too.

Time for Earth

Cole plants a tree. Trees give off **oxygen**. We need this to breathe.

Nora picks up **litter**. This helps keep our Earth clean.

What Do You See?

What kind of paper does Eli's class reuse?

18

Eli's class **reuses** paper. Reusing makes less waste.

People like to take time to help our Earth. How do you celebrate Earth Day?

Find Out More

BOOK

Landau, Elaine. *Celebrating Earth Day*. Berkley Heights, NJ: Enslow, 2012.

WEB SITE

PBS Kids: Sid the Science Kid
www.pbskids.org/sid/cleansup.html
Help Gabriela sort and recycle litter in the park!

Glossary

celebrate (SEL-uh-brate) to enjoy an event or holiday with others

litter (LIT-ur) bits of garbage

oxygen (AHK-si-juhn) a gas with no color that humans and animals need to breathe

reuse (REE-yooz) to use something again instead of throwing it away

Home and School Connection

Use this list of words from the book to help your child become a better reader. Word games and writing activities can help beginning readers reinforce literacy skills.

air	day	plants	waste
animals	Earth	reuse	water
begins	grow	special	work
breathe	learn	spring	
celebrate	litter	together	
class	oxygen	trees	
clean	planet	warmer	

What Do You See?

What Do You See? is a feature paired with select photos in this book. It encourages young readers to interact with visual images in order to build the ability to integrate content in various media formats.

You can help your child further evaluate photos in this book with additional activities. Look at the images in the book without the What Do You See? feature. Ask your child to point out one detail in each image, such as a color, time of day, animal, or setting.

Index

About the Author

Jenna Lee Gleisner is an editor and author who lives in Minnesota. She celebrates Earth Day by picking up litter in her community, planting trees, and recycling.